ORIGAMI SAFARI

Desert Animals

By Ruth Owen

WINDMILL
BOOKS

New York

Published in 2015 by Windmill Books, An Imprint of Rosen Publishing
29 East 21st Street, New York, NY 10010

First Edition

Produced for Rosen by Ruby Tuesday Books Ltd
Editor for Ruby Tuesday Books Ltd: Mark J. Sachner
Designer: Emma Randall

Photo Credits:
Cover, 1, 3, 5, 6-7, 8-9, 10-11, 12-13, 14-15, 16-17, 18-19, 20-21, 22-23, 24-25, 26-27, 28-29, 31 © Ruby Tuesday Books; cover, 4-5, 6, 10, 14, 18, 22, 26 © Shutterstock.

Library of Congress Cataloging-in-Publication Data

Owen, Ruth, 1967– author.
 Desert animals / by Ruth Owen. — First Edition.
    pages cm. — (Origami safari)
 Includes index.
 ISBN 978-1-6153-3908-2 (library binding) —
 ISBN 978-1-4777-9242-1 (pbk.) — ISBN 978-1-4777-9243-8 (6-pack)
1. Origami—Juvenile literature. 2. Desert animals in art—Juvenile literature. 3. Animals in art—Juvenile literature. I. Title.
 TT872.5.O933 2015
 736.982—dc23
                                    2014013949

Manufactured in the United States of America

CPSIA Compliance Information: Batch #WS14WM: For Further Information contact Rosen Publishing, New York, New York at 1-866-478-0556

Contents

Desert Origami

A **desert** is a dry **habitat** where very little rain falls each year. Most deserts are hot and dry, but some are cold and dry.

The ground in a desert can be sandy or rocky. Some deserts have no plants, while others have grasses, **cacti**, and other low-growing, **hardy** plants.

Surviving life in the desert is difficult, but many animals make their homes in this **environment**. In this book you can read about six animals that live in the desert. You will also get the chance to make a model of each animal using **origami**.

Cacti and other plants in a desert in Arizona

Origami Fox

In the hot, sandy Sahara Desert in North Africa, there lives a tiny desert animal with truly enormous ears. The little fennec fox is only the size of a small cat, but its ears can grow to be 6 inches (15 cm) long!

A fennec fox's ears radiate, or give off, heat from its body, helping to keep the fox cool. To protect its feet from the scorching-hot desert sand, it has thick fur on the bottoms of its feet.

By day, fennec foxes keep cool underground in **burrows** they dig in the sand. As the desert cools at night, these little animals leave their homes to **forage** for food such as **rodents**, insects, eggs, and plants.

YOU WILL NEED:
• To make a fox, one
sheet of yellow paper
• A marker

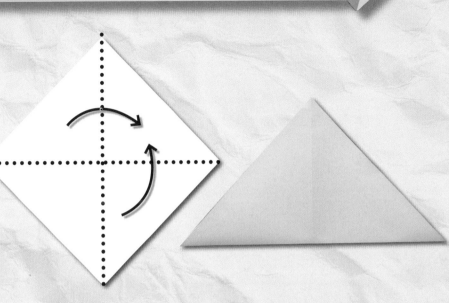

Step 1:

Fold the paper in half
diagonally, crease, and
then unfold. Repeat in the
opposite direction, and
crease to make a triangle.

Step 2:

Fold the right-hand point of
the triangle into the center,
and crease. Then repeat with
the left-hand point.

Step 3:

Flip the model over. Fold
the model in half, and
crease well.

Step 4:

Now turn the model so that the long side of the triangle forms the model's left-hand edge.

Long side of triangle

Step 5:

Next, fold back the right-hand edge of the model along the dotted line, and crease well.

Step 6:

Now open out the three layers of paper inside the fold you made in step 5.

Open out the layers

Flatten the two outer layers to make the fox's ears. The middle layer will form a pocket that becomes the fox's head and legs.

Ear

Head and legs

Ear

Step 7:

Gently squash down and flatten the pocket to make the head and legs, and crease well.

Head

Front legs

Step 8:

Using a marker, draw a face on your fox.

Step 9:

Finally, to help your fox stand up, fold in the left-hand point of the model.

Origami Rattlesnake

Many different **species** of snakes make their homes in deserts, including rattlesnakes.

These snakes get their name from the rattle on the ends of their bodies. The rattle is made from rings of a substance called keratin, which is the material that forms your fingernails. When a rattlesnake vibrates its rattle, the rattle makes a hissing sound. The snake makes this noise to scare away or warn off **predators**.

If the warning doesn't work, however, the rattlesnake may strike. In a split second, it will bite its attacker and inject **venom** into its enemy through its fangs. A rattlesnake also uses its venomous bite to kill the animals it feeds on.

YOU WILL NEED:

• To make a snake, a sheet of paper that's colored on one side and white on the other

Step 1:

Place the paper colored side down. Fold the paper in half diagonally, crease, and unfold. Then repeat in the opposite direction.

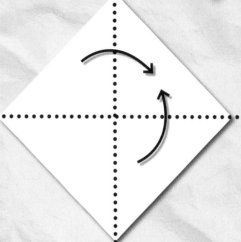

Step 2:

Fold the bottom point of the paper up to the center of the model, and crease. Then fold down the top point of the paper to meet the center, and crease.

Step 3:

Now make a new fold by folding up the bottom of the model so the bottom point meets the top edge of the model, and crease. Then return the bottom of the model to its original position. Now repeat the fold you've just made with the top point of the model.

Step 4:

Unfold the top point, then fold it back down again so it meets the top crease. Crease well.

Repeat on the bottom of the model.

Step 5:

Turn the model over. Now fold up the bottom point to meet the first crease (see dotted line). Then fold everything below the dotted line behind the model, and crease.

Fold up

Your model should look like this.

Now fold everything behind the model forward again along the dotted line. The snake's body is now starting to form.

Step 6:

Now using the snake's body as your guide, continue to fold the snake behind and then forward again, creasing well.

Step 7:

When you reach the center crease, repeat steps 5 and 6 on the top half of the model.

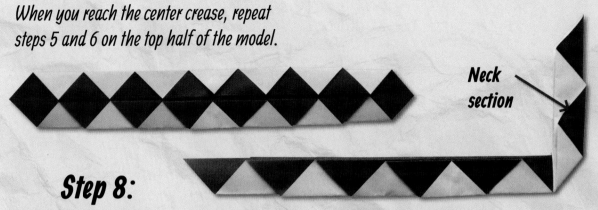

Neck section

Step 8:

Fold the snake in half. Now fold up one end of the snake to make a "neck" section, crease well, and unfold.

Open out the neck section, and then reverse fold it back on itself so that the neck closes around each side of the body.

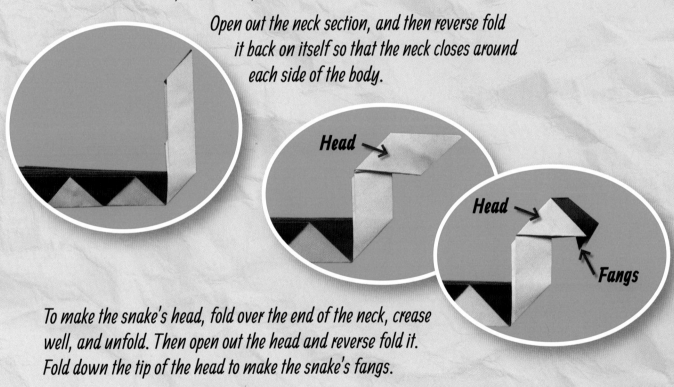

Head

Head

Fangs

To make the snake's head, fold over the end of the neck, crease well, and unfold. Then open out the head and reverse fold it. Fold down the tip of the head to make the snake's fangs.

Step 9:

Rattle

Finally, fold up and scrunch the end of the snake's body to create its rattle, and your snake is complete.

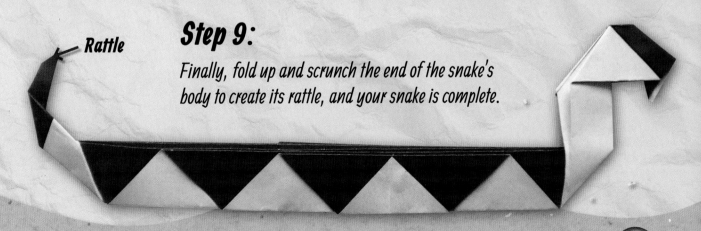

Origami Tortoise

Deserts are home to many types of reptiles, including tortoises.

Desert tortoises dig burrows in the ground with their shovel-like front legs and large claws. During the hot summer months, they stay underground in their burrows keeping cool. In winter, the desert can be freezing cold, so desert tortoises spend the winter months underground, too, keeping warm.

Scientists have estimated that desert tortoises spend about 95 percent of their time inside their burrows. They can go for months without food and water.

When spending time above ground in spring and fall, desert tortoises feed on grass and other plants. They even eat spiny cacti such as prickly pear plants.

Step 1:

Place the paper colored side down. Fold in half, and crease.

Fold in half again, and crease.

Step 2:

Now open up the top layer of paper to create a pocket.

Pocket

Gently squash down the pocket to form a square.

Step 3:

Turn the model over. Open out the triangle-shaped section of the model to create a pocket.

Gently squash down the pocket to form a square.

Open out here

Pocket

Step 4:

Fold in the left- and right-hand sides of the model along the dotted lines, and crease. You should only be folding the top layer of paper.

Step 5:

Fold down the top point of the model, and crease.

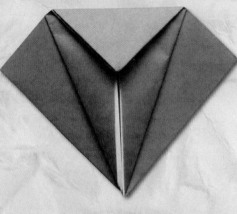

Step 6:

Now open out the folds you made in steps 4 and 5 to create a pocket.

Top point

Top point

Pocket

Take hold of the top point of the pocket and pull it backward while gently squashing and flattening the sides of the pocket to create a diamond shape.

Cut here

Step 7:

Now cut the top half of the diamond through its center along the dotted line.

Step 8:

Fold down the two points of the diamond to create the tortoise's front legs.

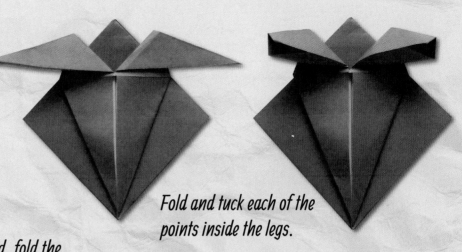

Fold and tuck each of the points inside the legs.

Step 9:

To make the tortoise's head, fold the top point of the model backward, and crease hard. Then fold the point forward again, making a small pleat.

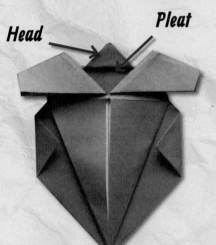

Head **Pleat**

Fold in the two sides of the model to create the tortoise's shell.

Step 10:

Fold out the two bottom points of the model to make the tortoise's back legs.

To make the tortoise's tail, fold in the bottom point of the model, and crease. Then fold the point back out again, making a small pleat.

Pleat

Tail

Step 11:

Flip the model over. If you wish you can draw a pattern on the tortoise's shell.

Origami Camel

There are two types of camels—Bactrian camels and dromedary camels. Bactrian camels have two humps and live in Asia. Dromedaries have one hump and mostly live in Africa and the Middle East.

Most of the world's dromedaries are **domesticated**. People living in deserts often use them to carry goods and as a means of transport.

A dromedary has several **adaptations** for life in the desert. Its hump can store many pounds (kg) of fat. When food and water are scarce, this fat is broken down by the camel's body to provide the animal with water and energy. When a **sandstorm** blows up, a camel's eyes are protected by bushy eyebrows and long eyelashes. The animal can also close its nostrils to keep out sand.

Step 1:

This project has lots of steps. The earlier steps follow the same design as the tortoise, so turn to page 15, and follow steps 1 to 6 of the tortoise model. At the end of step 6, your model should look like this.

Step 2:

Turn the model over. Fold in both side points, and crease well. Then fold down the small triangular flap in the center of the model.

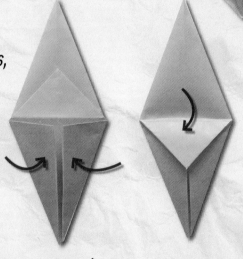

Next, open out the three folds you've just made to create a pocket (as you did on the other side of the model). Gently squash and flatten the pocket to create a diamond shape.

Your model should look like this, with the split section at the bottom.

Step 3:

Fold the top left-hand edge into the center along the dotted line, and crease well. You should only be folding the top layer of paper.

Turn the model over and fold the top right-hand edge of the model into the center. Crease hard.

Step 4:

Turn the model by 180 degrees. Fold down the top right-hand (and thicker) pointed section of the model, crease, and unfold.

Reverse fold

Now, using the crease you've just made, reverse fold the pointed section.

Step 5:

Fold down the top left-hand section of the model, crease, and unfold.

Reverse fold

Now, using the crease you've just made, reverse fold this section.

Step 6:

Turn your model over. It should look like this.

Now, to make the camel's front legs, fold down the center point of the model, and crease. Repeat on the other side. The hump will be revealed and your camel will now be taking shape.

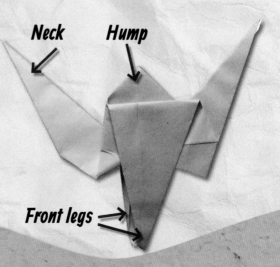

Neck

Hump

Front legs →

Step 7:

Fold back the neck section along the dotted line, crease hard, and then unfold.

Head

Reverse fold the neck

Using the crease you just made, reverse fold the camel's neck. Then fold over the top point of the neck to make the head.

Step 8:

Next, take hold of the right-hand pointed section of the model, open it out and start to fold it down. As you do, reverse fold this section into the camel's backside. This section becomes the camel's back legs.

Reverse fold in here

Finally, fold down the top, right-hand point of the camel's front leg on each side to smooth off the slope of the hump.

Fold down the front leg's point

To help your camel stand, you can fold under the tips of the legs to make feet.

Origami Tarantula

There are about 900 different species of tarantulas on Earth. Many species of these large, hairy spiders live in deserts.

The western desert tarantula can be found living in deserts in Arizona and Mexico. This spider can grow to have a leg span of 6 inches (15 cm) across.

A desert tarantula uses its legs to dig a burrow in the sandy ground. It surrounds the burrow entrance with silk that it produces inside its own body. If an insect, such as a cricket or a beetle, walks past the burrow and disturbs the silk, the tarantula feels this movement. Then it rushes from its hideaway and captures its **prey**.

Step 1:

Place the paper white side down. Fold in half along the dotted lines, crease, and unfold.

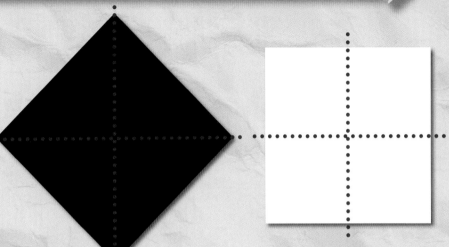

Turn the paper over. Fold in half along the dotted lines, crease, and unfold.

Step 2:

Place the paper white side down. When viewed from above, it should now look like this.

Pick up the paper, and using the creases you've just made, collapse in the sides of the model, as shown here.

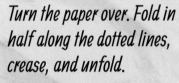

Collapse in here

Collapse in here

Squash down

Step 3:

Squash down on the model to form a square.

Step 4:

Take hold of the right-hand side point of the square (just the top layer of paper). Lift it up, open it out slightly, and then gently squash it flat to form an upside-down kite shape.

Right-hand point of model, lifted and opened out

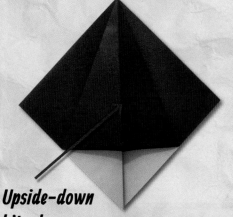

Upside-down kite shape

Now, opening and closing each of the other three sides of your model in turns, repeat what you've just done on the other three points until your model looks like this.

Step 5:

Next, working with just one diamond and the top layer of paper, fold each of the bottom edges into the center of the model, crease hard, and unfold.

Now gently lift up the section marked A to form a pocket. Then, using the creases you've just made, squash and flatten the pocket to create a small kite shape.

Small kite shape

Pocket

Again, move around your model, repeating everything you've done in step 5 three more times until your model looks like this.

Step 6:

Now open up your model at a flat section that contains no kite shape. Working with just the top layer of paper, fold the two sides into the center crease along the dotted lines, and crease hard. Now repeat on the model's other three flat sections.

Flat section with no kite shape

Your model should look like this.

Cut up the centre of each long point.

Step 7:

Your model will now have four long, pointed sections. Carefully cut up the center of each point to create eight points, or legs.

Open up the model to a section that contains a small kite shape, and begin folding the legs out to the side.

Two points (or legs) created by cutting

Step 8:

Fold some of the legs forward and some backward to create a realistic shape for your origami tarantula.

To round off the tarantula's body, you can fold the end point under.

Open out a section with a kite shape

Fold the point of the body under here

Origami Woodpecker

Gila woodpeckers live in deserts in Mexico and the southwestern United States. These birds use saguaro cacti as a place to build nests and find food.

When it's time for a woodpecker pair to breed, they make a hole in the stem of a saguaro cactus with their long, powerful beaks. Then the female lays between three and five eggs in the hole. Inside the cool cactus nest, the eggs and chicks are protected from the hot desert sun.

Many insects lay their eggs in the flesh of saguaro cacti stems. When **larvae** hatch from the eggs, gila woodpeckers feed on the fat, juicy young insects.

- To make a woodpecker,
  one sheet of yellow paper
- Scissors
- Red and black markers

Step 1:

Place the paper colored side down. Fold the paper in half, crease well, and then unfold. Fold the paper in half again, in the opposite direction, crease well, and then unfold.

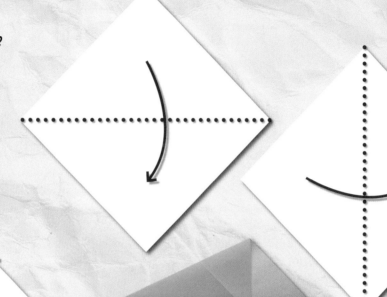

Step 2:

Fold the top and bottom points into the center crease along the dotted lines. Crease well, and then unfold.

Step 3:

Now fold the top and bottom points into the center crease in the opposite direction. Crease well, and then unfold.

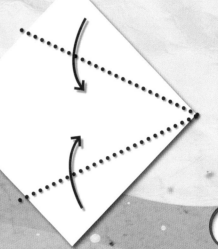

27

Step 4:

Now gently fold the top half of the paper into the center crease while allowing the top point to create a beak-like pocket. Then squash the pocket and fold it to the right-hand side of the model.

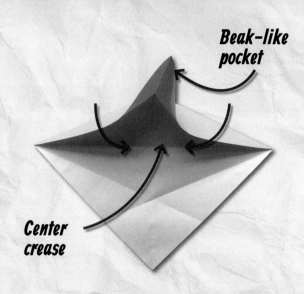

Beak-like pocket

Center crease

Squashed beak-like pocket

Repeat on the bottom half of the model.

Step 5:

Turn the model over. Fold down the top half along the center crease.

Step 6:

Turn the model by 90 degrees. To make the woodpecker's head, fold down the top point, crease well, and then unfold.

Open out the head section of the model.

Then using the crease you've just made, reverse fold the head so that the two halves of the head enclose the neck.

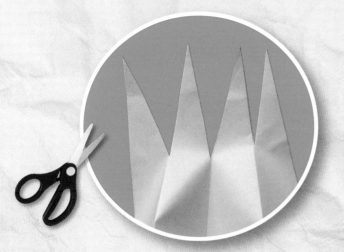

Step 7:

Now unfold the bottom, or tail, point of the model. Carefully cut it into four sections.

Step 8:

Fold out and arrange the four points you've just made to create the woodpecker's tail.

Step 9:

Finally, give the woodpecker a red patch on its head. Color the beak black, draw on eyes, and add black feathers to the wings and tail. Your gila woodpecker is complete!

Glossary

adaptations (a-dap-TAY-shunz)
Physical changes or changes in behavior that happen over time and make a plant or animal more able to survive in its environment.

burrows (BUR-ohs)
Underground homes used by animals. Some animals dig their own burrows, others use natural holes in the ground or the old, empty burrows of other animals.

cacti (KAK-ty)
Plants with sharp spines that grow in deserts and survive the dry environment by storing water in their stems.

desert (DEH-zurt)
A place that receives less than 10 inches (25 cm) of rain or snow each year. Deserts can be hot or cold. They are often sandy or rocky, with few trees and other plants.

domesticated
(duh-MES-tuh-kayt-ed)
Tamed by people.

environment (en-VY-ern-ment)
The area where plants and animals live, along with all the things, such as weather, that affect the area.

forage (FOR-ij)
To move from place to place looking for food.

habitat (HA-buh-tat)
The place where an animal or plant normally lives. A habitat may be the ocean, a jungle, or a desert.

hardy (HAR-dee)
Very tough and able to survive in an extreme environment.

larvae (LAR-vee)
Young insects that hatch from eggs and look like fat worms.

origami (or-uh-GAH-mee)
The art of folding paper to make small models. Origami has been popular in Japan for hundreds of years. It gets its name from the Japanese words *ori*, which means "folding," and *kami*, which means "paper."

predators (PREH-duh-turz)
Animals that hunt and kill other animals for food.

prey (PRAY)
An animal that is hunted by another animal as food.

rodents (ROH-dents)
Small mammals such as mice, rats, and squirrels.

sandstorm (SAND-storm)
A huge, fast-moving cloud of sand. Sandstorms happen when powerful winds pick up sand and carry it over land.

species (SPEE-sheez)
One type of living thing. The members of a species look alike and can produce young together.

venom (VEH-num)
A poisonous substance passed by one animal into another through a bite or sting.

For web resources related to the subject of this book, go to:
www.windmillbooks.com/weblinks
and select this book's title.

Read More

Allgor, Marie. *Endangered Desert Animals*. Save Earth's Animals. New York: PowerKids Press, 2013.

Clark, Willow. *Camels*. The Animals of Asia. New York: PowerKids Press, 2013.

de Lambilly-Bresson, Elisabeth. *Animals in the Desert*. Animal Show and Tell. New York: Gareth Stevens Publishing, 2008.

Index